Tracks

Memoirs from a Life with Music

Peter Cherches

BAMBOO
DART
PRESS

LOS ANGELES † NEW YORK † LONDON † MELBOURNE

Tracks: Memoirs from a Life with Music by Peter Cherches

ISBN: 978-1-947240-20-9

eISBN: 978-1-947240-21-6

First Printing 2021

For playlists with these songs (Spotify and YouTube) as well as other links, please visit cherches-tracks.blogspot.com

Author photo by Scott Friedlander.

For information:

Bamboo Dart Press

chapbooks@bamboodartpress.com

Curated and operated by Dennis Callaci and Mark Givens

Bamboo Dart Press 006

www.pelekinesis.com

www.bamboodartpress.com

SHRiMPER
www.shrimperrecords.com

Contents

For playlists with these songs (Spotify and YouTube) as well as other links, please visit cherches-tracks.blogspot.com

In memory of Harry Wittenberg, a fellow traveler.

The Beatles, "I Want to Hold Your Hand" (1963)

It was the musical perfect storm: Beatlemania and a pair of eight-year-old ears. I'm sure there are studies out there, but I instinctively think that's about the age we begin to form a real sense of our musical preferences, as we start to get both a refined sense of our own selves as well as our place in a social set and the cultural marketplace (even if we're not aware of it at the time). Music becomes essential to our identities as well as the soundtrack of our generation. If the studies say otherwise, I don't want to know about them.

This was the Beatles' first number-one hit in the U.S., and we got it a couple of months after the Brits. The group had earlier hits back home, like "Please Please Me" and "Love Me Do," but they charted in the U.S. a little later. By now it's pretty well known how Capitol Records, already owned by EMI, turned down the *Please Please Me* album, thinking it would never fly with the American market, so instead it was released, with a few tunes omitted (including "Please Please Me" itself) by Vee-Jay records, a Chicago indie label best known for some great rhythm & blues recordings, as *Introducing The Beatles*. I owned that record. It would be worth hundreds, if not thousands of dollars today.

Capitol got the message pretty quickly and started releasing Beatles singles and albums in the U.S. *Meet the Beatles* featured "I Want to Hold Your Hand." "She Loves You," which was actually the earlier hit of the two in the UK, appeared on their next U.S.

release, *The Beatles' Second Album*. For the most part, the original British albums have now become standard issue, but it's hard not to cling to the track configurations of one's childhood.

Of course, I was aware of a range of music before The British Invasion. I had two older brothers. From Harvey, who was eight years older, I'd hear records by the likes of The Four Seasons and Jay and the Americans (one of whom, Howard Kane, né Kirschenbaum, was related to the owner of our local funeral parlor, Kirschenbaum's, almost as exciting as the news that Mary Tyler Moore once attended the local Catholic school, St. Rose of Lima, which we pronounced like the bean). Bart, who was 12 years older, was as hypermusical as I'd become, and his bag was The Rat Pack and the Great American Songbook, a taste he shared with my mother, who had the radio tuned to WNEW-AM all day, home of "The Make-Believe Ballroom."

But once the Beatles hit the charts a portable radio was an essential accessory to the lives of myself and my friends. We'd have it tuned to WABC or WMCA while we played punch ball and stoopball and Chinese handball. For a more private listening experience in the pre-Walkman days you'd either have a mono earphone that looked like a hearing aid or you'd hold the speaker up to your ear. At night, you'd put the transistor radio under your pillow for surreptitious listening. That's how I heard Jean Shepherd's Saturday night routines from the Limelight club in Greenwich Village, one of my earliest storytelling influences.

I started spending most of my allowance on records, 45s and LPs, mostly by British groups. You name it: The Rolling Stones,

The Dave Clark Five (who for a while were almost as big as The Stones), Gerry and the Pacemakers, The Kinks, Manfred Mann, Herman's Hermits, The Zombies, The Animals. The Top 40 was a constant subject of kid conversation. For the most part, the only real competition for the British bands for a couple of years came from Motown. And there were always the megahit outliers, like Louis Armstrong's "Hello, Dolly" and Sgt. Barry Saddler's "The Ballad of the Green Berets."

One day in 1964 or '65, when he would have been about 20, my brother Bart took me on a record-buying expedition to Sam Goody's. When we brought my albums to the checkout, the cashier, a middle-aged man, said to Bart, "Cute kid. Is he your son?"

Miles Davis, "Straight, No Chaser," from *Milestones* (1958)

One of the first jazz albums I bought as an adolescent, I think when I was 12, was *Milestones*, by the Miles Davis Sextet. I figured I'd kill two jazz birds with one stone: Miles Davis and John Coltrane, neither of whom I'd ever heard, to my knowledge. I was unaware at the time of the more legendary status of the group's next album, *Kind of Blue*. I did know that Miles Davis was possibly the most famous living jazz musician, and that Coltrane had a reputation for playing really "weird." Weird interested me. I understood weird. I was a weird kid.

When I looked through the bin for Miles Davis albums, most likely at Sam Goody's, *Milestones* caught my eye. On the cover was Miles in a green shirt, sleeves rolled up, holding his trumpet, staring straight out at me. He looked like he meant business. On the back cover I read that the album featured Coltrane on tenor sax, as well as Cannonball Adderley, whom I knew from his radio hit "Mercy, Mercy, Mercy," on alto. I was unaware that it also featured one of the greatest rhythm sections in jazz history. In fact, I was most certainly unaware of the term "rhythm section." It looked like a good bet. I bit.

I really liked the album, but something confused me: Coltrane didn't sound weird at all. He sounded like a pretty normal jazz saxophonist. At the time I knew nothing of the phases of Coltrane's career. I would listen to the album over and over and try to figure out what the uproar about Coltrane was all about.

All right, maybe there was a little something I could latch on to, maybe something in his tone, maybe something in the runs he played (he was in the midst of what jazz critic Ira Gitler called his "sheets of sound" period). But I wasn't convinced there was anything so revolutionary about Coltrane.

Over the next few years I got to know a lot more about Coltrane, and how his playing kept changing over the decade from 1957 until his death in 1967. In 1970 I was visiting my brother Bart at his bachelor pad and I started twisting the dial on the FM tuner of his stereo system. I came across some really intense jazz, a saxophonist seemingly blowing his brains out in the best of ways (I'd soon learn that there were other saxophonists who blew more brains further out). It turns out I had stumbled upon the multi-day Coltrane festival on WKCR, the radio station of Columbia University. That was my crash course in Coltrane, and, as I became a devoted listener of WKCR, in all sorts of jazz, but especially free jazz. In 1971 I bought Coltrane's *Live in Seattle* double album, which was recorded in 1965 but had just been posthumously released. *That one* was too much for me.

I ultimately made peace with *Live in Seattle*, but after all these years I still can't get into certain of Coltrane's late albums, *Om*, for instance, which may have been recorded under the influence of LSD or may just sound like it was. When I first heard it, I figured the guy had totally lost it. All these years later I've come to understand that I just haven't found it yet. And that I might never. And that's all right.

Mountain, "Theme from an Imaginary Western," from *Climbing!* (1970)

The first rock concert I attended without family chaperones was Mountain, at the Fillmore East, when I was 14, along with some friends from junior high. I was to learn many years later that the opening act, Ambergris, a horn-oriented group in the mold of Chicago and Blood, Sweat and Tears, included two of the greatest future Jewish salsa musicians—keyboardist and bandleader Larry Harlow (aka El Judio Maravilloso) and trombonist/violinist Lewis Kahn (no relation to architect Louis Kahn). Speaking of Jews, I had no idea at the time that Leslie West was Jewish. Little Leslie Weinstein. Actually, I doubt he was ever little.

By the time of the concert, West had two albums under his belt. Technically, the first album, called *Mountain*, was a West solo album, and *Climbing!* was released after his group had been named Mountain. I wouldn't lose any sleep over it if I were you.

For the most part the band played pure hard rock, built around West's gritty power guitar and vocals. But "Theme from an Imaginary Western" broke that mold. Composed by Jack Bruce and his lyricist partner Pete Brown, the song originally appeared on Bruce's solo album *Songs for a Tailor*. But it got wider exposure in the Mountain version, with vocals by bassist Felix Pappalardi, who had co-produced the Bruce album. The song features one of the most beautiful melodies of the classic rock era, a startling counterpoint to the album's big hit, the hard-rock onslaught of

"Mississippi Queen." You know what I mean?

This was the first of a number of concerts I attended at the Fillmore. That first time I think I was straight, or on weed at most, but at subsequent concerts I was often on psychedelics.

The concert I remember most was the one where Elton John opened for Leon Russell. I loved Russell's music, on his own albums as well as with Joe Cocker, and John was, of course, at the beginning of his career, which was the beginning of the end for me—but I did love his eponymous album and *Tumbleweed Connection*, which was released in the U.S. a few months after the concert.

There were also the big disappointments. A show where Fleetwood Mac opened for Van Morrison was a total disaster. It was the transitional Fleetwood Mac lineup—with John McVie's wife Christine Perfect as vocalist—reunited with the band's founder, guitarist Peter Green, who was already deep into his mental health issues. The set was a total train wreck. And Van was a major bringdown too. He performed the entire show mumbling his lyrics into his shoes. Morrison has a reputation as a very uneven live performer, and, having seen him three times over a 30-year period, I can attest to the veracity of that. Two of those shows sucked, one was great.

Then there was the show where John Mayall had to apologize. It was supposed to be a program with three bands featuring amplified violins. It's a Beautiful Day performed their big song "White Bird." The Flock, with future Mahavishnu Orchestra violinist Jerry Goodman, performed their song "Big Bird." I don't think Mayall had any bird songs. His group was supposed to feature the great Don "Sugarcane" Harris on violin, but by the time of the show Harris was out. The set was abominable, I mean bad trip abominable, so much so that after his penultimate tune, Mayall announced, "I realize we were fucking awful, but we're going to try one more before we go," something like that, definitely the "fucking awful" part.

During Mayall's fucking awful set I was tugging on my rubber face as the walls of the Fillmore East began to close in on me.

The Partridge Family, "Come On, Get Happy – The Partridge Family Theme" (1970)

I have a confession to make. When I was 14 and 15 I would, from time to time, watch *The Partridge Family*. Not because I liked the show, or the music, no, I had no interest in the show and I thought the music was really lame, bullshit bubblegum. I mean, seriously, I was listening to Mountain and Ten Years After! No, I watched the show for one reason alone: Susan Dey, who played Laurie Partridge. I had the hots for Susan Dey. Susan Dey gave me hard-ons, or, to use somewhat more clinical terminology, she fueled my masturbatory fantasies. I only half paid attention to the show, waiting for Susan Dey's on-screen moments.

Of all my TV and movie heartthrobs, Susan Dey was one of the few who was fairly close in age to me, though she was still four years older. Maureen McCormick, who played Marcia on *The Brady Bunch*, was more my contemporary, a few months younger than me, but Maureen McCormick was decidedly Avis to Susan Dey's Hertz.

Elizabeth Montgomery, in *Bewitched*, was probably the first. *Bewitched* debuted in 1964, when I was eight, so I surely wasn't getting Samantha Stevens hard-ons at first, but the show did have an eight-year run.

Among film actresses, I had developed crushes on Lee Remick and Ann-Margret, the beginning of a lifelong "thing" for redheads.

Even the cartoon Ann-Margrock on *The Flintstones* thrilled me. In the older films I'd see on TV, I was especially moved by Rita Hayworth. Oh, and Rhonda Fleming. Lovely Rita! Help me, Rhonda!

But back to the matter at hand, Susan Dey. I remember the time I went to a candy store in a nearby neighborhood to buy a special Partridge Family issue of *Tiger Beat*, for jerkoff material, of course. I certainly wasn't going to buy it at any of the candy stores where I was known, Fred and Rudy's, Zee Gee, or Gus's, because what if word got out? So I went a few blocks further to a candy store where I was an unknown quantity and furtively purchased that issue of *Tiger Beat*, as well as a pack of Jujubes to help cover my real motive.

Actually, I'm pretty sure that's a false memory.

The Temptations, "I Wish It Would Rain" (1967)

Before Stevie Wonder and Marvin Gaye ushered in the label's *auteur* period, my favorite Motown recordings were by The Temptations. For me, The Temps managed to put across a grittier, more soulful style than most of the other groups on Gordy's labels, thanks largely to David Ruffin's lead vocals that could have held their own at Stax, along with the goose-bump-inducing falsetto of Eddie Kendricks.

At first, Smokey Robinson was the group's producer and principal songwriter, composing most of their early songs, including the first one I remember hearing on the radio, "My Girl," their first number one hit, at the end of 1964.

Another Motown writer/producer, Norman Whitfield, felt that he could make The Temptations even bigger, so he asked Berry Gordy for the opportunity to work with the group. Gordy liked to foster a spirit of competition among his stable and gave Whitfield the chance to prove himself after the Smokey-penned "Get Ready" failed to break the Top 20. Gordy told Whitfield that if he could produce a single that would outperform "Get Ready," the group was his. Whitfield's song was "Ain't Too Proud to Beg," which made number 13 on the pop chart and number one on the R&B chart. The group was his.

Most of Whitfield's songs for The Temptations featured lyrics by Barrett Strong, who had recorded Motown's first hit single, "Money (That's What I Want)," but several were written with another lyricist, Rodger Penzabene, including one of the best, "I

Wish It Would Rain."

Penzabene had written lyrics for an earlier Temptations song, "You're My Everything." That song was inspired by Penzabene's wife, with whom he was head over heels in love. Alas, not long after that, Penzabene discovered his wife was cheating on him. Terrible for the psyche, but fodder for one of the great modern torch songs. The prevailing conceit, the weather motif, common enough in popular music ("Stormy Weather" anyone?), is worked out eloquently and consistently, from a simple but powerful beginning: "Sunshine, blue skies, please go away." The jilted lover doesn't see stormy weather, he wants stormy weather, so his pain can blend in.

Once, at a rehearsal, I asked my collaborator Lee Feldman, an excellent lyricist in his own right, what qualities he thought made for a great lyric. He said strong visual imagery was the thing he most looks for, the picture that can crystallize the sentiment.

> Day in, day out, my tear-stained face
> Pressed against the window pane.
> My eyes search the skies, desperately for rain.

Positively cinematic, no? A man (who "ain't supposed to cry") crying at the window, cursing the beautiful day, yearning for an external manifestation of his inner misery in the weather, a kind of cosmic companionship as well as convenient camouflage for his tears.

The record was released in late December of 1967. A week later, on New Year's Eve, Rodger Penzabene committed suicide.

Johnny Winter/Ten Years After, "Good Morning Little Schoolgirl" (1969)

I was one of the many kids who got turned on to the blues by listening to white rock bands playing covers of black blues records. Sometimes the same tune would be covered by multiple groups, and "Good Morning Little School Girl" gained traction with quite a number of them. It's credited to Sonny Boy Williamson (the first Sonny Boy Williamson), who recorded it as "Good Morning, School Girl." By 1969 we had heard lots of rock covers of blues classics, first by The Rolling Stones, The Animals, and The Yardbirds, then Canned Heat and Cream, among others, but by the time I turned 13 I was ready to pursue the originals, and it was the rock records that pointed me in the right direction.

The versions of "Good Morning Little School Girl" by Johnny Winter and Ten Years After were released within months of each other, but their takes on the song, both certainly rooted in the blues, were quite different. Winter's rendition was closer to classic electric Chicago blues and featured a horn section, while the Ten Years After version was more in a hard rock or psychedelic vein, with jam band inclinations (theirs is about three times as long as Winter's). For me the Winter version sounds much less like a period piece now. But the Ten Years After recording, featuring the pyrotechnics of guitarist Alvin Lee, was huge among the crowd I hung out with, not least for the vocal refrain "I want to ball you,

I want to ball you all night long." Teenagers are very impressed by musical pyrotechnics (as well as balling), and we devoured Ten Years After's *Ssssh* album that included the tune.

Winter was certainly capable of guitar pyrotechnics of his own, but his first Columbia release is a wonderfully eclectic album of blues and blues-oriented styles. It includes a version of "Drown in My Own Tears" that hews very closely to Ray Charles' recording, an electric cover of B.B. King's "Be Careful with a Fool," and a solo acoustic rendition, in pure Delta style, of Robert Johnson's "When You Got a Good Friend." The Robert Johnson revival got another push when The Stones featured "Love in Vain" on *Let it Bleed* later that year. In 1961, Columbia had released the Johnson compilation *King of the Delta Blues Singers*, and this was the source of his repertoire for most of those white bands, but "Love in Vain" wasn't on that one, so in 1970 Columbia released Volume II, the first Robert Johnson collection I bought. The first track of Johnson's I'd heard was his "Little Queen of Spades," on a 1969 twofer from Columbia, *The Story of the Blues*, a tie-in with Paul Oliver's book of the same name.

The Story of the Blues was quite a resource for a young blues novice, featuring mostly pre-WWII acoustic blues of all regions and styles. If it was weak on electric blues (Elmore James' "Sunnyland" being one of the few electric tracks), I could, and did, augment it with a fantastic series of three albums called *Chicago/The Blues/Today!* that Vanguard had released a few years earlier.

I became a blues-mad adolescent, feverishly collecting records from all corners of the blues. And I also caught up on the British blues bands I had missed a few years earlier, like the original Fleetwood Mac and John Mayall's Bluesbreakers. Mayall was really big among my friends at this time, due to the breakthrough popularity of his album *The Turning Point*, especially the track "Room to Move." I remember one kid saying to me, "You know, Mayall's really old, man. Thirty-seven!"

Hank Williams, "Lovesick Blues" (1949)

Most of us lived in Midwood and Kensington, but we'd go to Park Slope to drink. This was when I was 18–21 years old, right before 21 became the legal drinking age in New York. I think I drank more in those few years than the rest of my life put together. In the mid-seventies, Park Slope was full of bars (when I bought an apartment there in 1988 most of them had become realtors). Sometimes we'd go to The Gaslight, occasionally The Coach Inn or Snooky's or City Lights, all within a half mile of each other on 7th Avenue, but most of the time it was The Iron Horse, where a guy played ragtime on a broken-down upright piano on weekends, and between his sets we'd pump coins in the jukebox. I can't remember what records were on the box except Hank Williams' "Lovesick Blues," which was a favorite of the bartender, Greg. We'd sit there for three to five hours on a Friday night, drinking nonstop. Blaine (our designated driver!) drank the most, tossing his signature boilermaker, shots of Scotch with screwdriver chasers, all night; he'd often sing (or slur) along with the Hank Williams record. At one point, a year or two into our tenure there, Greg, who was gay, convinced the owners to make the place into a gay-friendly bar, which pretty much meant just that and not much more, except that one night a very "straight-looking" white-haired guy in a black business suit tried to pick up one of my friends, the only time something like that happened. It was sort of a half-assed gay bar.

When we were done drinking, usually around midnight or 1AM, four or five of us would pile into Blaine's car and drive to Chinatown, where we'd usually go to Wo Hing, an old-style Cantonese rice shop on Pell Street that stayed open until 4AM. Among our favorite dishes were Singapore chow mei fun and squid with black bean sauce, but sometimes we'd get congee (rice gruel), which was a pretty good drunkard's dish. One of our crowd, the younger brother of Steve, one of my *Zone* magazine co-editors, would always order the same thing, mixed congee. Then he went off to college in California. He returned to Wo Hing on a break from school a couple of years later, his first time there since he'd left town. He reported back that when he entered the restaurant one of the waiters said to him, animatedly, "Mixed congee! Where you been?"

Sam Rivers Trio, "Ecstasy," from *Paragon* (1977)

For a group that worked together so long and so intensely, recordings by the trio of Sam Rivers, Dave Holland, and Barry Altschul are surprisingly few and generally obscure. The only other album I'm familiar with by this trio (outside of the three musicians appearing together in other groups) is *The Quest*, from the previous year. I think the three of them first appeared together on Dave Holland's landmark ECM album *Conference of the Birds*, from 1973, which also featured saxophonist Anthony Braxton.

From 1974–76, the trio was more than a group I saw many times, they were part of a coming of age for me. The setting for most of those encounters was Sam Rivers' own loft, Studio Rivbea, on Bond Street in lower Manhattan. Rivbea, named for its patron saints Sam and his wife Bea, was the epicenter of the loft jazz movement, in which a number of free-jazz-oriented players like Rivers, percussionist Warren Smith, drummer Rashied Ali, singer Joe Lee Wilson, and saxophonist Charles Tyler, among others, took a DIY approach to presenting their own music and that of kindred spirits when jazz itself had lost much of its commercial viability and there was little room in the established clubs for the more "outside" players.

On a typical Friday or Saturday night, when I normally went to Rivbea, Sam's trio (or another one of his groups like Winds of Manhattan) would split a bill with a guest artist's group. For most of the time I attended, the shows were held in the basement space, which was not air-conditioned. We sat on cushions on the floor.

The only time I remember it being oppressively hot and crowded was when Sam's trio split the bill with Anthony Braxton's quartet. Both groups shared the rhythm section of Dave Holland on bass and Barry Altschul on an expanded drum kit, including cowbells, temple blocks, and sirens.

Upstairs one could take a break and buy refreshments or Bea's homemade fish sandwiches, though toward the end the stage had moved upstairs. Bond Street, which is home to hip restaurants these days, was pretty industrial and quiet after dark back then. It would be some years before the neighborhood was dubbed Noho. The Rivers' landlord was Robert De Niro's mother.

A performance by Rivers' trio was more a flow than a set, usually an improvised suite without any break between sections. Though Sam was primarily a wind player (tenor and soprano saxes and flute), he also played piano and would move among his instruments. The deep listening and interplay of the three musicians kept me riveted. With jazz at its best, the group itself is an organism, and this trio was a prime example of that.

Sam and Bea were the most gracious of hosts to the musicians and the listeners. Sometimes I went with friends and sometimes I went alone, but one was never alone in that audience of mostly hardcore devotees of some of the most vibrant music of the time. Conversations would spontaneously erupt. For me, at 18–20 years old, this world of mostly African-American musicians taking charge of the presentation of their music without compromise was an education in artistic integrity that has stayed with me all my life.

Mark Murphy, "Stolen Moments," from
Stolen Moments (1978)

What exactly makes a singer a "jazz singer?" To paraphrase Justice Potter Stewart, "I know it when I hear it."

Mark Murphy was, to my ears, the quintessential jazz singer. I first became aware of him when his *Stolen Moments* album came out in 1978, by which time I was already familiar with most of the better-known jazz singers. Murphy's original lyrics to Oliver Nelson's jazz standard quickly became popular with jazz radio deejays (I first heard it on New York City's WRVR). I could immediately tell that this guy had mastered the entire jazz vocalist's toolkit.

Murphy was a fearless singer. He took the kinds of chances that would sound ridiculous on lesser artists. His rhythmic fluidity was virtually unparalleled among male singers, and his scat singing convincing even to a scat skeptic like myself. Murphy would treat the changes of a tune like a lover in a complicated relationship: he might caress them at first, settle into them, and then challenge them, push them—playfully, of course. He could bend a tune, a lyric, to his will while knowing full well he was still respecting the composition, in his own sweet way. Murphy stretched the limits of a song while maintaining the integrity of the melody and lyric even as he radically altered what was written.

The *Stolen Moments* album finds Murphy really climbing the

peaks after a nearly 25-year recording career. Its repertoire represents just about all aspects of Murphy's art: original lyrics for jazz tunes, vocalese (a standout is a version of Annie Ross's lyrics for the Wardell Gray tune "Farmer's Market"), sublime ballad performances ("We'll Be Together Again," a favorite among jazz singers, and the lesser known "Again"), and the Brazilian repertoire he would continue to explore with more sensitivity than any other English-language singer, represented here by Jobim's "Waters of March" and Dori Caymmi's "Like a Lover."

While my natural reticence, not to mention my technique, is certainly not up to the audacity and exuberance of Murphy's performances, I nonetheless consider him a vocal role model. I once took my older brother Bart, who was my mentor through osmosis of The Great American Songbook when I was very young (i.e., I listened to the records he was listening to), to a Mark Murphy gig at the club Fat Tuesday's. Bart, who was up on the extended Rat Pack (including the third cousins twice removed) and all the saloon singers, wasn't really that familiar with many of the hardcore jazz singers, so Murphy was new to him. During the performance, I could see that Bart was really into it. After the set, he enthused, "Murphy's the best! How did I not know about him all these years?"

João Bosco, "Papel Machê," from *Gagabirô* (1984)

This happened in London on the morning of November 5, 1999. I know the date because I still have the program from the concert I attended that evening, one of the most amazing shows I've ever seen.

I had come to London to see the concert "Since Samba Has Been Samba," named for a song by Caetano Veloso ("Desde Que o Samba É Samba"). It was an all-star Brazilian show at the Royal Albert Hall, a benefit for an organization that aided Brazilian street urchins.

I first fell in love with Brazilian music when I was ten, when the Sergio Mendes and Brasil '66 version of Jorge Ben's "Mas Que Nada" was a hit. My full immersion in Brazilian popular music started around 1984, after seeing a concert by Milton Nascimento at Carnegie Hall. I had known of Nascimento through his work with jazz saxophonist Wayne Shorter. After that concert, looking through the Milton Nascimento section of a record store bin, I came across an album of his songs performed by the singer Elis Regina. Elis was arguably the greatest female vocalist of Brazilian pop, but I was unfamiliar with her at this time. Well, that album really sealed the deal for me. I fell head over heels for her voice, and I started buying up all of her records I could find. Elis was huge in Brazil, and she helped launch the careers of the post-Tropicália generation of singer-songwriters by recording their tunes: Milton, Djavan, Ivan Lins, and the team of João Bosco and Aldir Blanc. The Bosco-Blanc songs moved me in particular, so I started buying all of João Bosco's albums.

The show at the Albert Hall featured six of Brazil's most famous singers, three men and three women: Caetano Veloso, Gilberto Gil, Chico Buarque, Gal Costa, Elza Soares, and Virginia Rodrigues. The concert featured each of the artists performing solo, then duo, relay-style. So, for instance, Gilberto Gil sang some songs, then Gal Costa came on for a duet with him, then she sang solo, then Caetano came on for a song with her, etc. There was also a special guest, British hipster icon Georgie Fame, who had a couple of American hits in the sixties, "Yeh Yeh" and "The Ballad of Bonnie and Clyde." I believe it was the first time I'd seen any of these artists, and the opportunity to see Chico Buarque live was a special treat, as he had performed very rarely for quite a long time, devoting more time to his second career as a novelist. The show was also a homecoming for Caetano and Gil, who had lived in London from 1969–72, in exile from the junta. Caetano sang his song "London London" to thunderous applause.

I was staying at a small hotel near Hyde Park. I noticed at breakfast that most of the kitchen staff were Brazilian. I think this is common in London hotels. I got into a conversation with the guy who was serving me. I told him about the concert I was going to see that evening, and he was incredibly envious. He became nostalgic about Brazil and Brazilian music. He sat down at my table to chat, probably breaking the rules.

"I love all these singers," I told him, "but one singer I really love who is not on the program is João Bosco." I had just seen Bosco live for the first time the previous year, at Lincoln Center.

"Oh, João Bosco, I love him too. His song 'Papel Machê' was very special. So beautiful." The song, a romantic ballad, was a breakthrough hit for Bosco in 1984. I saw tears begin to well up in the waiter's eyes. "I really miss Brazil so much," he said, his voice cracking, pining for his sunny homeland, so far away, on this typically gray, damp, November morning in London.

Steve Lacy, "Micro Worlds," from *Clinkers* (1978)

Among casual jazz fans, the soprano sax is certainly most associated with John Coltrane, who took the instrument up in 1960 and was first heard playing it on "My Favorite Things," one of his best-known recordings. After that it became almost a requirement for tenor saxophonists to double on soprano, and most followed Coltrane's approach, where the instrument took on the flavor of an exotic Eastern double-reed instrument.

The father of soprano sax playing in jazz was the early New Orleans master Sidney Bechet, who was also the first influence on Steve Lacy, the indisputable modern master of the instrument, Coltrane notwithstanding. Lacy started out playing Dixieland, but by the mid-fifties he had become utterly engrossed by the music of Thelonious Monk, eventually joining Monk's band for a few months, and had started working with the likes of Gil Evans and Cecil Taylor as well, ultimately becoming one of the brightest lights of the jazz avant garde.

But during the sixties and seventies, when the intensely emotional outpourings of free jazz represented the main strain of jazz's outer limits, Lacy was fashioning an approach that was more cerebral and analytic, a direction that surely grew out of his deep involvement with Monk's music. His mastery of an instrument that by all accounts presents myriad difficulties, not the least of which being the challenge to play it in tune, was consummate. He set out to discover everything his chosen instrument was capable of revealing (he played no other horns).

In the seventies Lacy started performing solo concerts, where he'd explore the sonic possibilities of his instrument. The album *Clinkers*, recorded at a concert in Switzerland, is one of the earliest documents of this work. It is most assuredly not easy listening. While he does perform a tune or two that he also recorded with his groups, like the opening track, "Trickles," each performance is a deeply analytical yet tactile engagement with the properties of the soprano sax, employing extended techniques and often eschewing any traditional tonality.

The track titled "Micro Worlds" is a prime example of this approach. While it most likely refers to microtonality, it also suggests to me a soundtrack of literal and imaginary micro worlds, be they entomological or microbial. At the beginning it appears to be one of the tamer cuts, opening with a simple, plaintive melody, but then things begin to change drastically; at first, Lacy interweaves a continuation of that melody with high pitches broken by occasional guttural punctuation, and soon the melody is history. Way beyond the official upper range of the instrument, he slides around notes and sounds like a figure skater from another galaxy. Some might be tempted to reach for a can of 3-in-One oil, but I find the performance wholly engaging. Finally, Lacy comes in for a landing, a very brief restatement of that simple melodic figure.

Yet even if his cerebral inclinations were dominant, Lacy was not without his warm and tender moments. Perhaps the best example of his romantic side is a program of Ellington and Strayhorn compositions he recorded in a duo with a frequent collaborator, pianist Mal Waldron, on the album *Sempre Amore*. Still, neither Lacy nor Waldron drop their edge completely.

I never got to see a Steve Lacy solo concert, but I saw him perform with groups of varying size, including a duo performance with Waldron. The last time I saw him perform, in 2003 at the Iridium club in New York, with a group that featured Lacy's wife, the violinist and singer Irene Aebi, it was a fraught occasion due to the inside knowledge I was privy to through a friend of Lacy's, an acquaintance of the friend I attended the gig with. Earlier that day Steve had been diagnosed with liver cancer (also the cause of Coltrane's death). With that information, the looks of tenderness and concern on Irene's face during the set had a secret meaning for those of us in the know. Ironically, Lacy had been planning to go into the studio to record his first duo album with his longtime bassist Jean-Jacques Avenel, who several years earlier had been diagnosed with cancer too, I believe of the stomach. Lacy was concerned that the clock was ticking against that project due to Avenel's illness, but the bassist survived the saxophonist by ten years.

After the set was over, I noticed another acquaintance in the audience, an amateur soprano sax player himself. He had brought a stack of Lacy LPs for autographs. I went up with him to meet Lacy. As Steve was going through the albums he got to *Clinkers*. "That's a rare one!" he said.

"Rare but well done," I said.

He smiled. "Rare but well done, I like that."

That wasn't, however, the last time I saw him. The last time, probably weeks before his death, Lacy was an audience member for a solo piano concert by Ran Blake, another true original, a former colleague at The New England Conservatory of Music. Such a memorable last view of a great artist in his final days, smiling as he enjoyed the music of a friend who also pursued a unique musical vision.

Chris Smither, "No Love Today," from *Live as I'll Ever Be* (2000)

I could have written this piece about any of a number of artists or songs, because what I want to talk about is the joy of discovering a new artist in live performance. By new, I mean new to the listener.

Chris Smither was just a name to me when I decided to catch his set at Seattle's Bumbershoot Festival in 2001. Just about all I knew about him was that he had roots in the sixties folk scene, something I was never really into. What I got was a consummate fingerstyle guitarist, a fabulous lyricist, and an engaging storyteller, both in his songs and his on-stage banter.

Smither grew up in New Orleans, but he established his career in the coffee houses of Cambridge, MA. When I saw him he'd been at it for 35 years. And it was love at first song. His set included what has become my favorite Smither song, "No Love Today," which was also on the CD I bought after the set was over.

Smither introduces the song with memories of itinerant produce sellers in New Orleans who would call out their wares in musical cadences. He interjects that the vegetable known in Louisiana as mirlitons are known elsewhere as chayote, a kind of squash.

The song is partly in the voice of one of these fruit and vegetable hawkers. He announces what he's got, and what he hasn't: He's got bananas, watermelon, peaches, sweet corn, okra, and mirlitons, but he's got no love today.

And then, at the end of the song, Smither sums it all up so beautifully:

> In the end no one will sell you what you need,
> You can't buy it off the shelf,
> You got to grow it from the seed...

Still, I could have written about Jimmie Dale Gilmore, the Austin-based singer-songwriter who's also part of the group The Flatlanders, and whom I first saw and heard that same weekend in Seattle; his songs and singing were so honest and direct that I bought his latest CD too.

Or Dominican jazz pianist Michel Camilo, who was a special unannounced guest at a concert put on by the Caribbean Cultural Center in New York, just as his first CD was being released, and who wowed everybody with his prodigious technique, the joy of his compositions, and his sweet charm and humility.

Or maybe those opening acts I ended up preferring to the main attraction.

When you go to see an artist you love, or are at least familiar with, you tend to view the show through the lens of your expectations. Did they do the music you thought you were going to hear? How did it compare with previous performances? If they were taking a new turn, were you going along for the ride or were you disappointed in this new direction?

But when you see an artist about whom you have no preconceived notions, and they're good, really good, it's a kind of high, the joy of a newfound love. I think there are really different things that are happening to you physically and emotionally when this transpires.

I sometimes complain about having to sit through mediocre opening acts when I'd rather just see the artist I came for and get home earlier, but then one of those opening acts turns out to be a real revelation, a new musical love for life, so you've got to take it as it comes.

So get out of your comfort zone of the familiar. Check out artists you've never seen or listened to before, "some that you recognize, some that you've hardly even heard of."

Drupatee, "Mr. Bissesar" (1988)

One of the things we've lost in the age of streaming, where music from the world over is available at a click, is the joy of the hunt. Once upon a time, any foreign travel I did always involved a search for local music not readily available in the U.S. I'd buy cassettes in shops or from street sellers and listen to them on a Walkman, to immerse myself in the sonic flavors of the place. Sometimes I'd do prior research, sometimes I'd ask for recommendations.

In South India I bought tapes of U. Srinivas, the teenage prodigy who played Indian classical music on an electric mandolin and would later join John McLaughlin's Indo-Jazz fusion group Shakti, as well as some Malayalam (the language of the state of Kerala) devotional music that featured western-sounding vocal harmonies that I'd never previously heard in Indian music.

In Malaysia I bought recordings of dangdut, the Indonesian and Malay style that's mostly a fusion of Arabic pop and Indian film music.

In Bangkok I bought a tape by a rock group I'd read about in a book about the changing face of Southeast Asia. I couldn't remember the name of the group, so I went to a record store and said, "I can't remember the name, but I'm looking for tapes by a rock band that uses Thai folk music as the basis for their songs." The sales person smiled and nodded, "Ah, I think you mean Carabao." He put one of their CDs on for me in a listening booth, like U.S. record stores used to have. I liked it and bought a cassette. Sometimes I'll hear their music in a Thai restaurant and surprise the staff when I ask if it's Carabao.

In Portugal I found a little shop by the beach in Estoril where a guy was selling tapes of African pop from the former Portuguese colonies. This was territory I was already familiar with, especially Cesária Évora from Cabo Verde and Bonga from Angola, but this guy had all sorts of great stuff that was new to me, like Bana, a male vocalist from Cabo Verde who was as big as Cesária back home, and Ruy Mingas, one of the pioneers of Angolan pop music. The seller was Portuguese, but he had grown up in Angola and was an evangelist for the music. He was thrilled by my interest. "I'm European," he said, "but I also consider myself African."

Sometimes my hunts were at the behest of a writer friend, M. Kasper, who was also a fan of then-obscure forms of world music. Once, when I was planning a trip to Washington, D.C., he asked if I could find any recordings by the Ethiopian singer Aster Aweke, since the area has such a large Ethiopian community. It turned into a fun safari. First I went into a big record store by Dupont Circle and asked a clerk if they had any recordings by the Ethiopian singer Aster Aweke. "We don't," he said. "I think your best bet would be to go to the Ethiopian restaurants in Adams Morgan and ask around. Sometimes they sell cassettes." So I did just that. I had no luck at the first place, but at the second restaurant a guy told me, "There's a social club nearby where you can buy tapes," and he wrote down the address. I went to the address, walked up some stairs, and found myself in a room where a bunch of young Ethiopian guys were hanging out shooting pool. I asked the bartender if they sold tapes by Aster Aweke. "We do," he said, and I discovered that they had duplicating equipment in the back room where they'd make copies of tapes. I don't know what kind of financial arrangement, if any, they had with the artists, but I bought a couple of cassettes for my friend.

One of my favorite travel finds was also at Kasper's behest. I was going to be in Port of Spain, Trinidad, at the end of 1989 and he had asked if I could try to find some tapes of chutney, also known as Indian soca, the fusion of calypso and soca with Indian rhythms, instrumentation and cultural references. "I'm most familiar with Babla and Kanchan," he said, "but I'm sure there must be lots more." Indeed there was. I found a place that sold mixtapes. For myself, I bought a tape of the year's top soca hits, and one of parang, the traditional Trinidadian Christmas music that's sung in Spanish with a Trini accent and played on the cuatro, a small guitar that's popular in Caribbean Latin America. For Kasper and myself, I bought a couple of copies of an Indian soca mixtape. It was really fun music. My favorite tracks were "Mister Bissesar" by Drupatee, one of the most popular chutney singers, and a song called "Curry Tabanca," which opened with this unforgettable couplet:

> She pack up all her curry and she run away,
> Leaving me to worry myself sick each day.

Lawrence D. "Butch" Morris, "Conduction 58," from *Holy Sea Vol. 1* (1999)

Butch Morris was a true American original, a musical artist of singular genius and originality whom I'm confident posterity will speak of in the same breath as Charles Ives, John Cage, and Duke Ellington, even if he's far from a household name today. Butch came out of the jazz tradition, but well before his death in 2013 he had gone way beyond the boundaries of genre.

Butch started out as a brass player, a cornetist, but his real legacy is the work he did in a form of his own devising, Conduction, which grew out of an ever-searching musical vision. He came to New York in the mid-1970s from Southern California, along with a number of other musicians who were welcomed into the vibrant jazz loft scene: David Murray, Arthur Blythe, Butch's brother Wilber (a brilliant bassist), and a then-unknown drummer and writer named Stanley Crouch, who would abandon his adventuresome roots to become a dyed-in-the-wool jazz neocon. Butch was one of the first of the musicians from the loft world to start collaborating with some of the younger musicians working within a new, eclectic "downtown music" vocabulary, among them John Zorn, Wayne Horvitz, and Bobby Previte. Around the same time a new kind of music started welling up inside his head, and he studied conducting in order to realize what he was imagining. Over time, Butch's concept gelled, at first with musicians from familiar circles, but eventually the entire world became his musical oyster.

The simplest description of Butch's Conduction is structured improvisation. He developed a series of gestures, a language that would be used in rehearsals and performance to create new and unpredictable music with various groups of improvising musicians from many traditions, collaborative composition in real time. The phrase may be a cliché, but it was always a musical tightrope walk, and truly, to risk another cliché of the jazz world, "the sound of surprise."

Part of the joy of watching a Butch Morris Conduction, besides his hand gestures and, of course, the musicians, was watching Butch's face. I don't know if the facial expressions were part of the official language of Conduction, but they could certainly be meaningful. Most of the time, as I remember, the expression was one of focus, but on occasion the scowl would show itself, and what a formidable scowl it was. But my sense is that the scowl, aimed at one musician or another, didn't mean, "You fucked up," it didn't mean, "You're screwing up *my* music," it meant, I'm pretty sure, "My friend, you're letting yourself down." Because Butch always set the highest standards for himself and for all the musicians he worked with. He was a teacher, in the rehearsal room and on the bandstand, in the great jazz tradition of Duke Ellington and Charles Mingus. And then there was the smile, that big, beaming mother of all smiles that would suddenly appear on the Morris visage, a smile that maybe meant something like: "I'm pleased," "This is all coming together," "I'm proud of you," "Thank you," and, no doubt, "I love you."

Musicians from the jazz world and other improvising traditions cherished the opportunity to work with Butch, but once he started getting commissions there could sometimes be friction and resistance. My favorite story in this vein involves a performance that became the double-CD set *Holy Sea*, with the Orchestra della Toscana. Butch had received a commission to work with this Italian chamber orchestra, and these classically trained musicians, for whom improvisation was an alien concept, were not happy campers at first. They goofed off, showed up late for rehearsals, flaunted their disdain and generally kept their hearts out of the project. How did Butch react? He took the musicians aside and said something to the effect of, "If you guys sound like shit, it's your problem, not mine. I'm just a visitor here. When I leave here and move on to my next project, this will be behind me, but you live here, you'll have to face this audience again, so what shall it be?" It worked. The musicians shaped up, fell in love with the process, all the acrimony dissolved, and it turned out to be one of Butch's most successful Conductions.

I knew Butch Morris, casually, for just over 30 years. We met on January 25, 1982, pre-Conduction. I was producing and hosting a show at Symphony Space called "A Benefit for Nothing," which was a benefit for the "Nothing Issue" of my magazine, *Zone*. Butch was supposed to appear with writer Jessica Hagedorn, but Jessica had to be in Manila for a funeral, so Butch did a solo cornet performance. After that, I'd often run into him in the East Village, our mutual neighborhood until I moved in 1987, and we'd exchange quick hellos, usually accompanied by the abundant

Butch Morris smile. Same quick hellos and smiles when I'd check in with him after a Conduction. I once ran into him, somewhat incongruously, I thought, at an early Norah Jones show. But Butch was musically voracious.

I'm pretty sure the last time I saw him was at a screening of the excellent documentary about Butch and Conduction, *Black February*. Afterwards I went up to him and said, "Butch Morris, star of stage and screen."

"Oh, come on!"

Bobby "Blue" Bland, "Ain't Nothing You Can Do" (1964)

One of the most exciting shows I've attended was at a samba club in Salvador, Bahia. Salvador was my favorite of four stops in Brazil, and I stayed in the old heart of the city, Pelourinho. I'd read that it was a dangerous, high-crime area, but once I settled in it didn't seem at all frightening. In my three days there, there was nothing that felt like a close call. It's a fascinating area of down-at-the-heels colonial architecture, great African-influenced food, and music everywhere, much of it for free at outdoor venues. I was in heaven, Brazilian music being one of my great passions. One evening I saw a free concert at an open-air venue that featured an Afro-Brazilian percussion ensemble. When I left that show, I saw that there was a music club across the street. I had studied Portuguese for the trip, so I asked the guy at the door, "O que tipo de música?" He replied, "Samba!" I bought a ticket.

I went through the doorway, and it was a big club, with many tables, already full. Even though there was a façade, it was an open-air space, a shell of a building. I took an empty table toward the back. The other audience members and the musicians were various shades of black, and I don't think there was one white, or even "moreno," Brazilian in the audience. The program featured a number of groups, and I think it went on until the wee hours; I caught three different bands before I left at around midnight. I was intoxicated by the scene, the high-energy music, the people mingling and dancing. A couple of times people passed my table, smiled, and offered a greeting, but mostly I just sat and took it all in and sipped my cerveja, beaming with joy.

One time in Chicago, in the 1980s, I went to a blues club on the West Side, the roughest part of town, the poorest African-American ghetto. I was in town to do a show, and one of my cohorts had a friend who was playing harmonica in the band, a white guy. We parked the car about a block away, saw lots of burnt-out buildings, and several people on the street cautioned us, "You folks take care of yourself around here." The club looked like a classic juke joint, and when we, a group of five or six young white people, came through the door, all eyes turned toward us. Those eyes belonged exclusively to middle-aged and older Black people. Immediately, a short, gray-haired man, went over to a table and spoke to the people sitting there. They got up, smiling, not looking at all put out, and the guy started wiping the table with a cloth. We all felt a little weird about displacing the other customers, but we got the vibe that they wanted us to feel at home. The performer was Tail Dragger, a Howlin' Wolf protégé, who sang in a gravelly voice as he slithered along the floor, snakelike. Audience members kept coming by to say hello and ask how we were doing. The man who got us the table introduced himself as Top Hat and danced with the two women in our party. It turned out that Top Hat didn't even work there; he was just one of the regulars.

I saw the great blues singer Bobby "Blue" Bland two times in the 1990s. The first time was at Kimball's East, in Emeryville, in the Bay Area. Not only was Bland's audience at the club almost exclusively Black, it was almost exclusively African-American women "of a certain age," his natural constituency. Years earlier I had read about Bland's hypnotic sex appeal in Charles Keil's book *Urban Blues*. Almost all the tables were occupied by groups of six to eight women in their 50s and up.

Bobby "Blue" Bland did not disappoint. He had the audience in the palm of his hand. Women were swooning, occasionally making their pleasure audible. At one point, between tunes, Bobby was kibbitzing and said, referring to me and one young couple, "I see a few white people in the house tonight. Well, that's all right!"

Louis Armstrong, "Beale Street Blues," from *Plays W.C. Handy* (1954)

I went to Memphis and didn't visit Graceland.

First of all, I'm really not that interested in Elvis, and I just wasn't up for taking a half day to make a pilgrimage to his gaudy shrine, no matter how de rigueur a tourist stop it is. I wasn't interested in the conspicuous consumption, the artifacts, or encounters with true pilgrims whose visit wasn't at all ironic.

I did, however, visit W.C. Handy's birthplace.

I was in town for the 2001 Memphis in May Beale Street Music Festival, which was held at a long, narrow park on the Mississippi River. I was especially interested in the older regional blues and R&B acts, but there were also some big-shot headliners at the two main stages, at opposite ends of the park. I saw Bob Dylan, my only time, and ran into a former coworker, who said, "He must have a strange form of Alzheimer's; he remembers the lyrics, but not the melodies." Other artists I caught included Mavis Staples, who was exquisite, as expected, Mississippi singer-guitarist R.L. Burnside, who played the rawest of acoustic blues, George Clinton and P-Funk, Willie Nelson, Steve Earle, Koko Taylor, and Ike Turner & The Kings of Rhythm, featuring a sexy young tail-feather-shaking chick singer with long conked hair who was clearly a Tina clone.

Beale Street itself, though the historic Black entertainment district, had by then become a sanitized tourist zone, but it was still home to A. Schwab's, originally a dry goods store that dated back to 1876, and where, in addition to notions and sundries and pots and pans, you could also find the voodoo supplies that were the stuff of blues lyrics, like John the Conqueror root.

Unlike Graceland, the W.C. Handy House is a humble shotgun shack. It houses lots of memorabilia of the "father of the blues," composer of "St. Louis Blues," "Memphis Blues," "Yellow Dog Blues," and lots of other songs with "Blues" in the title. I was the only visitor the afternoon I stopped by, so I had a chance to chat with the docent. She was an elegant, older, silver-haired African-American woman. She told me that her late husband had been the publisher of *The Chicago Defender*, America's preeminent Black-owned newspaper. She had moved to Memphis, where she had relatives, only a few years earlier. "Before I came here, we looked down our noses at the blues," she said. "We considered it unrefined. But since I've been here I've learned that it's really a very rich art form that our people should be proud of."

Sergey Penkin, "Feelings," from *Holiday* (1991)

I've only gone on one full-fledged, organized tour, one week in the Soviet Union, three nights each in Moscow and Leningrad. The deal was too good to pass up. The tour, offered by Pan Am Holidays, cost a total of $1,500.

This was during the final days of the Gorbachev regime, and his reforms were in full swing. The trip took place around Orthodox Easter, and for the first time in Soviet history services were being televised on Russian television. Also on TV, much to my surprise, was a gender-bending male vocalist named Sergey Penkin, who wore eye makeup, a pair of earrings, and sequins, and sang "Feelings" in English, modulating from a rich baritone to an extreme falsetto, changing the refrain at one point to "I'm feeling so gay." That line is not in his recording of the song.

The hotels were pretty awful, and we took most of our meals at them. Breakfast was especially dreadful because we couldn't get a decent cup of coffee.

One day, toward the end of the trip, I was strolling down the Arbat, Moscow's famous pedestrian-only shopping street, with two women from the tour, sisters from Akron or Columbus or Toledo, somewhere in Ohio that wasn't Cleveland or Cincinnati. We had been lamenting the dearth of decent coffee. A few minutes later, as if by divine providence, I smelled the most wonderful, intense, fresh-ground-coffee aroma. "Do you smell what I smell?" I asked the women, wondering if I was hallucinating.

"Coffee!" they said, in unison.

"We have to find out where it's coming from," I said. Like some cartoon character, I began to follow the scent, leading with my nose. I was on the right track, because the aroma kept getting more intense. Finally we reached Mecca. It was a dark little coffee bar with an Italian-style espresso machine. I couldn't believe my luck.

I had taken a surprisingly effective two-day Russian for Travelers class at the New School, so I had a few phrases and a little vocabulary under my belt, and at the time I preferred to drink my coffee with milk. "U vas jest coffee s'malako?" I asked. ("Do you have coffee with milk?")

"Nyet, tolka chorniy," the counter man replied. ("No, only black.")

So I ordered a black coffee. What I got was a full cup of intense, delicious espresso, a triple at least. I can't remember how many rubles or kopeks it cost me, but it was incredibly cheap, something like a quarter.

Later that day, at Red Square, we saw the long line outside GUM, the giant department store, where people waited hours to shop for they knew not what.

Anton Webern, "Six Bagatelles for String Quartet, Op. 9" (1913)

I'm not particularly knowledgeable about classical music, and my tastes are somewhat limited and specific: Haydn quartets, Mozart piano concertos, Schubert lieder, the piano works of the Spanish late Romantics Granados and Albéniz, and especially music from the first half of the 20th Century: Bartók, Stravinsky, Debussy, Ravel, Satie.

Of all forms in classical music, I find the string quartet the most compelling. Recently I stopped to wonder what it was about the quartet that explains its hold on me. I found, in of all places Wikipedia, an uncharacteristically purple explanation that made perfect sense to me, though it appears the Wikipedia community was taken aback by the tone, and now only snippets remain in the entry. Luckily, I found the full passage on The Wayback Machine.

"With four parts to play with, a composer working in anything like the classical key system has enough lines to fashion a full argument, but none to spare for padding. The closely related characters of the four instruments, moreover, while they cover in combination an ample compass of pitch, do not lend themselves to indulgence in purely colouristic effects. Thus, where the composer of symphonies commands the means for textural enrichment beyond the call of his harmonic discourse, and where the concerto medium offers the further resource of personal characterization and drama in the individual-pitted-against-the-mass vein, the writer of string quartets must perforce concentrate on the bare bones of musical logic. Thus, in many ways the string quartet is pre-eminently the dialectical form of instrumental music, the one most naturally suited to the activity of logical disputation and philosophical enquiry."

That anonymous Wikiteer had crystallized it for me: The string quartet, in its very essence, displays the attributes I am devoted to in my own writing.

I'm particularly fond of Webern's "Six Bagatelles for String Quartet." Yet I've never been otherwise drawn to the work of the Viennese school of serialists to which Webern belongs, along with, most prominently, Schoenberg and Berg. I hardly know any of the music of the other two. As a matter of fact, I hardly know that much Webern, and there's hardly that much Webern to know; I think his entire published output clocks in at under four hours. But oh those Bagatelles.

I'm guessing I first heard the work at 19, in a 20th century music course I took as an undergrad. It immediately appealed to and furthered an austere aesthetic I was already developing. The drama that arose from Webern's restraint, his use of space and silence along with the relationships among the notes and other sounds produced by the strings, perhaps hinting at conversation, and the utter idiosyncrasy of it all, somehow reminded me of another artist who had captured my imagination not long before and helped me to focus the direction in which I wanted to take my writing: Harold Pinter.

The six movements run between about a half minute and a

minute and a half each, for a total of about four to five minutes, depending on the performance. I don't know how much of that time is accounted for by silence.

Webern's piece inspired the title of what I consider my breakthrough as a writer, a sequence of short prose pieces I called "Bagatelles," written in 1980 and first published as a letterpress chapbook the following year. It also appears in my 2013 collection of short prose sequences, *Lift Your Right Arm*, that title being the first sentence of "Bagatelles." The collection's title was kind of chosen for me by fate, as the first piece in the sequence is surely my best-known piece of writing, having been featured on Poetry 180, the website Billy Collins put together when he was U.S. Poet Laureate, featuring a poem by a living writer for each day of the school year. As the individual sections of "Bagatelles" didn't have titles, Billy listed my piece as "Lift Your Right Arm."

An artist I admired from yet another art form, Piet Mondrian, was as much an influence as Webern and Pinter. I had consciously set out to make writing that echoed the aesthetic of Mondrian's grid paintings. I originally conceived of the sequence as "relationship studies." I decided to use an ostensible relationship between a couple of two-dimensional characters, only referred to as I and she, as a narrative strategy to mirror the forms and sounds of those minimalist works that inspired me. These characters have no history beyond their relationship, no physical attributes, just the things they say to and about each other individually and as a union.

I wrote "Bagatelles" while I was working on my MFA in fiction writing at Brooklyn College. A component of the program was that, along with workshops, each student would do an individual tutorial with a faculty member. John Ashbery had agreed to work with me, I think, because my prose work fell between the cracks of genre (I don't call it poetry because it derives from a distillation of prose fiction), and he also had liked some translations of French poetry (Apollinaire and Eluard) I had published in the college literary magazine. Every other week, for a half hour or 45 minutes, I'd have a one-on-one meeting with John. We'd go over the pieces I was writing for "Bagatelles," but he also gave a writing assignment each time. They were often based on the techniques of the surrealists or the fixed forms of the Oulipo group, two areas of mutual interest. My writing, with its spare simplicity, was perhaps 180 degrees away from Ashbery's much more oblique style, or at least 90, but we shared a lot of literary interests. And I have to say that as a young writer it meant a lot to me to have the approval of a writer of his stature and intelligence. I still cherish, as one of the greatest compliments I've ever received, a comment he made about "Bagatelles": "This work is frighteningly simple."

The original ending of "Bagatelles" was:

What would you do if I died, she said.
Bury you, I said.

But I replaced it with the cheerier:

I created you out of nothingness and I can annihilate you any time I feel like it, I told her.
I'd like to see you try, she said.

I was 25 when I published "Bagatelles," and much of my subsequent writing derives from it. I like to think I've continued to do work of the same caliber, but I can't honestly say I've ever written anything better.

In an appreciation of the Webern composition, Arnold Schoenberg wrote, "Consider what moderation is required to express oneself so briefly. Every glance can be expanded into a poem, every sigh into a novel. But to express a novel in a single gesture, joy in a single breath—such concentration can only be present when there is a corresponding absence of self-indulgence."

Thelonious Monk, "Blue Monk" (1952)

In college I was working toward becoming a playwright, studying with Jack Gelber, best known for the play *The Connection*. Most of my literature courses were in drama, from the English, Comparative Literature, and Classics departments, and I took a number of courses in the Theatre department too. My professor for history of theatre was Benito Ortolani, a scholar of classical Japanese theatre, with a secondary focus on Western antiquity. Ortolani was as Italian as they come. He had a thick accent and his hands were in constant motion. One day a student asked him, "Professor Ortolani, how many languages do you speak?" He replied, "Seven living-a ones and two dead-a ones." In Ortolani's class I learned about the surviving ancient Greek theatre at Epidaurus, a magical place that since then had always had a bookmark in my brain.

It was close to 40 years later that I finally got to Greece. From Nafplio, a beautiful coastal city on The Peloponnese, I took a tour to Epidaurus.

The theatre was built at the end of the 4th Century BCE, not long after the death of Euripides, whose plays were surely performed there, along with those of Aeschylus and Sophocles. It's famous for its acoustics, a marvel of ancient engineering. Our tour guide pointed out that if you stand in the center, at ground level, and speak at a normal conversational volume, your words will be heard in even the highest, furthest seats—and the theatre seats about 14,000 spectators. "Try it," she told us. A couple of people went down and spoke a few words. What was I going to do? Here I was at a veritable shrine of the theatre world, long a destination of desire for me; I certainly wasn't going to say something banal like, "Hello, everybody!" Then I had a brainstorm.

My life in the arts has taken a number of twists and turns. By my senior year in college, it became clear to me that short fiction, rather than drama, was my true métier as a writer. By the early eighties I was doing what people were calling performance art, mostly monologues based on my own texts. Then I started working with musicians, and that inspired me to get serious about singing, so I studied for about five years with a fabulous jazz singer, Nanette Natal. In 1987 I did my first concert as a jazz singer, at the New York alternative music space Roulette. For the show, I had written lyrics for 18 of Thelonious Monk's compositions. Now I'd take the opportunity to consecrate Epidaurus with the music of Thelonious Monk.

So when my turn came I started singing my lyrics to "Blue Monk." I had finished one chorus when a security guard came up to me, sternly wagging her finger, saying, "No singing!" I stopped, but I should have said, "And what the hell do you think the Greek chorus did?"

I tell people that singing Monk at Epidaurus was the closest thing this atheist Jew has ever had to a "spiritual" experience. I hadn't really sung for close to 20 years, and this inspired me to get back in the game.

The Byrds, "Turn! Turn! Turn! (To Everything There Is a Season)" (1965)

I took a fairly long break from creative pursuits, beginning in 1992, when I started a doctoral program in American Studies at NYU. Of course, I did a fair amount of academic writing, and my dissertation was eventually published by a respected scholarly press, but for about 15 years I did almost no fiction writing. It was an even longer break from singing, about two decades. Then the urges returned, and I eventually plunged headlong back into both. I suppose there really is a season to everything. Or two.

"Turn! Turn! Turn!" came out at the end of 1965, when I was nine, and I read somewhere at the time that the lyrics came from the biblical book of *Ecclesiastes*, which I pronounced in my head as Excellecstasies, having never heard the word spoken.

I wanted to find out where in *Ecclesiastes* the lyrics could be found, so I got the bible down from the bookshelf over the telephone stand—for some reason we had one, a bible that is, though I can't remember anybody ever touching it before The Byrds came along—and looked in the table of contents. I found *Ecclesiastes*, but how was I going to find the lyrics to "Turn! Turn! Turn!" if I didn't want to read the whole damn thing? I don't remember whether the article I had read listed chapter and verse, but even if it did I wouldn't have had the slightest idea what to do with that intelligence. I figured I'd just skim, looking for the words "Turn! Turn! Turn!" But no matter where I turned, "Turn! Turn! Turn!" never turned up. Luckily I stumbled on what did appear to be the lyrics when I saw "To every thing there is a season, and a time to every purpose under the heaven." Actually, it wouldn't have been those exact words; that's from the King James Version; we had a Jewish bible. No matter, that's not the point. I did, after all, find what were, for the most part, the lyrics to "Turn! Turn! Turn!"

Except there was no damn "Turn! Turn! Turn!"

Billie Holiday, "I Cover the Waterfront" (1944)

I was very close with my maternal grandparents. They lived in an apartment in the same building as we did, and I'd often go upstairs to visit them, or to stay with them when I needed a babysitter. They died within a year of each other, in their mid-eighties, in the late sixties.

My grandma we called Gran, and my grandpa we called Pop. Gran called Pop Pop, and Pop called Gran Mama.

Both were Russian Jews, but Gran came to Boston when she was three years old and had a Boston accent without a trace of Russian. She was a thin, slight, perennially sweet woman who didn't have a bad word for anybody. Pop came to New York when he was a young man, to avoid military service, and retained a thick Russian accent. He was a short, fat, bald man, about five-foot-seven and 250 pounds. There was an old photo of him smoking a cigar, from the thirties, where he was the spitting image of Al Capone. He was a curmudgeon who hardly ever had a good word for anybody—except Mama, to whom he was devoted.

They both started failing around the same time and ended up in a nursing home. I know that Gran died before March of 1969 and that Pop died after, because Pop, who had entered a deep depression, claimed he was holding on only so he could be at my Bar Mitzvah. Pretty much all Pop ever said after Gran died was, "She was a saint," with tears in his eyes. Then he died a few months after the Bar Mitzvah, having nothing left to live for. He weighed 97 pounds.

After they had both died, we went upstairs (nobody gives up a rent-controlled apartment in New York) to go through their effects and see what there was to keep. I found a cabinet full of 78 RPM records. The only one I can remember was the Billie Holiday disc on the Commodore label that featured "I Cover the Waterfront" on one side and "Lover Come Back to Me" on the other.

I was already curious about jazz and blues, and I had certainly heard of Billie Holiday, but I'm pretty sure I had never actually heard her. I *had* heard her song "God Bless the Child" in the version by Blood, Sweat & Tears, but can't remember if I even knew it was her song (and the total mismatch of song to singer and arrangement still gives me the willies). Back then many turntables still had the 78 speed and could take a reversible cartridge, because the 78s took a thicker stylus than the one for "microgroove" recordings. I didn't have a 78 needle for my turntable, so I played the record with a standard one, which worked, but could ruin the grooves. And that's how I heard Billie Holiday for the first time, on a crackly 78 played with the wrong kind of needle.

It grabbed me. I instantly understood why Billie Holiday was considered such a great singer. It just sounded so natural. I enjoyed both sides of the record, but especially "I Cover the Waterfront," which suggested to me the surreal image of a giant literally covering a waterfront. I learned years later that the song was inspired by a novel and film of the same name. In the song it's a woman waiting by the waterfront, likely in vain, for her lover's return, presumably by sea. In the film it's a journalist whose beat is the waterfront.

The first Billie Holiday album I owned was a double LP of her thirties recordings on Columbia called *God Bless the Child* that came out in 1972. It featured an earlier recording of "I Cover the Waterfront" where Lady Day sang the song's verse, but she dispensed with it on the later recording for Milt Gabler's independent Commodore label (Gabler would soon become her producer at Decca). For me those 1944 Commodore recordings represent a sweet spot in her career. She was between contracts with John Hammond at Columbia and with Decca, where she was given more of a pop treatment than the pure jazz of her earlier records. Her voice was in fine form, and her interpretations fell somewhere between the youthful verve of many of the Columbia records and the weathered, battle-scarred, simmering intensity of her fifties work.

When I think back upon it, I'm really pleased that I found that record in my grandparents' collection, that I was able to discover Billie Holiday that way. I have no memories of my grandparents' musical tastes, and it fills me with joy to imagine them listening to Lady Day together, Gran's ear cocked toward the Victrola, listening intently, and Pop gazing lovingly at Mama, even if it never actually happened that way.

About the Author

Called "one of the innovators of the short short story" by *Publishers Weekly*, Peter Cherches has lived his creative life in the literary, music, and performance worlds of New York City and beyond for over four decades, as writer, editor, performance artist, singer, and lyricist.

His writing has appeared in scores of magazines, anthologies and websites, including *Transatlantic Review*, *Harper's*, *Bomb*, *North American Review*, *Fiction International*, *Fence*, *Little Star*, *High Times*, *Hambone*, *Semiotext(e)*, and *Poetry 180*. Poet Billy Collins wrote, "To Gödel, Escher, and Bach we might consider adding Peter Cherches." He has published three volumes of short prose with Pelekinesis since 2013: *Lift Your Right Arm*, *Autobiography Without Words*, and *Whistler's Mother's Son*. In addition, he has published three limited-edition letterpress artist's books with Purgatory Pie Press: *Colorful Tales*, *Mondrian-Tac-Toe*, and *Unfamiliar Tales*.

In the 1980s, Cherches was a fixture on New York's downtown music scene. Sonorexia, his collaborative "avant-vaudeville" band with multi-instrumentalist Elliott Sharp, performed at such venues as 8BC, Darinka, Club 57, King Tut's Wah Wah Hut, CBGB, The Mudd Club, and Folk City. They released a cassette, *It's Uncle!*, in 1985, now available digitally.

In 1984 he also began collaborating with keyboardist and songwriter Lee Feldman, writing original songs and performing monologues with improvised synthesizer soundtracks they called "Movies for the Ears." They have appeared at a wide range of venues in New York City, including La MaMa, The Knitting Factory, The Cat Club, St. Peter's Church, Cornelia Street Cafe, The Duplex Cabaret, and The Lone Star. Cherches and Feldman continue to work together to this day.

Peter Cherches started performing jazz in 1987, singing his original lyrics to compositions by the likes of Thelonious Monk and Bud Powell with some of the top jazz players from New York's downtown scene. His first album as a jazz vocalist, *Mercerized! Songs of Johnny Mercer*, featuring Lee Feldman on piano, was released in 2016.

112 N. Harvard Ave. #65
Claremont, CA 91711
chapbooks@bamboodartpress.com
www.bamboodartpress.com

CPSIA information can be obtained
at www.ICGtesting.com
Printed in the USA
BVHW011439080521
606653BV00017B/489